# BEST FRIENDS BOOK

By Sharon McCoy and Sheryl Scarborough

Additional material by Roxanne Camron

Illustrated by Charlene Olexiewicz

LOWELL HOUSE JUVENILE

LOS ANGELES

*NTC/Contemporary Publishing Group*

Published by Lowell House
A division of NTC/Contemporary Publishing Group, Inc.
4255 West Touhy Avenue, Lincolnwood (Chicago), Illinois 60712 U.S.A.

Copyright © 1999 by NTC/Contemporary Publishing Group, Inc.
All rights reserved. No part of this work may be reproduced, stored in a retrieval system, or transmitted in any form or by any means, electronic, mechanical, photocopying, recording, or otherwise, without the prior permission of NTC/Contemporary Publishing Group, Inc.
Requests for such permissions should be sent to the address above.

Managing Director and Publisher: Jack Artenstein
Director of Publishing Services: Rena Copperman
Editorial Director: Brenda Pope-Ostrow
Project Editor: Roxanne Camron
Designer: Treesha R. Vaux

Library of Congress Catalog Card Number: 99-73103

ISBN: 0-7373-0225-9

Lowell House books can be purchased at special discounts when ordered in bulk for premiums and special sales. Contact Customer Service at the address above, or call 1-800-323-4900.

Printed and bound in the United States of America

ML 10 9 8 7 6 5 4 3 2 1

# CONTENTS

Introduction . . . 4

## Chapter 1
What Friendship Is All About . . . 6

## Chapter 2
Friendship Challenges . . . 14

## Chapter 3
Resolving Pal Problems . . . 21

## Chapter 4
Gifts and Crafts for 4-Ever Friends . . . 33

## Chapter 5
Things to Do with You-Know-Who! . . . 49

## Chapter 6
Everything I Ever Wanted to Know About My Best Bud . . . 67

# Introduction

*A friend is a person with whom you dare to be yourself.*
—Author Unknown

Do you remember the first time someone told you that you were her best friend? Maybe it was in kindergarten and your friendship is still going strong. Or maybe that friendship changed and you've gone on to make other best friends.

No matter how long you've been best friends with someone, no one can make you feel better than a true friend can. Friends cheer you up, cheer you on, make you laugh, share your darkest secrets. For most girls, best friends and close friendships are what make life so special and fun. Packed inside these pages you'll find lots of useful info to keep your friendships on track. You'll learn what friendship is all about, and we'll tell you how to solve your biggest problems. You'll find out what to look for in a best friend and how to be a better friend yourself. Plus you'll find quizzes to take, crafts to make, and fun things to do—all with friendship in mind.

Whether you read this book from cover to cover or flip to the sections you're most interested in, *The Ultimate Best Friends Book* will help you and your friends enjoy the best friendships ever.

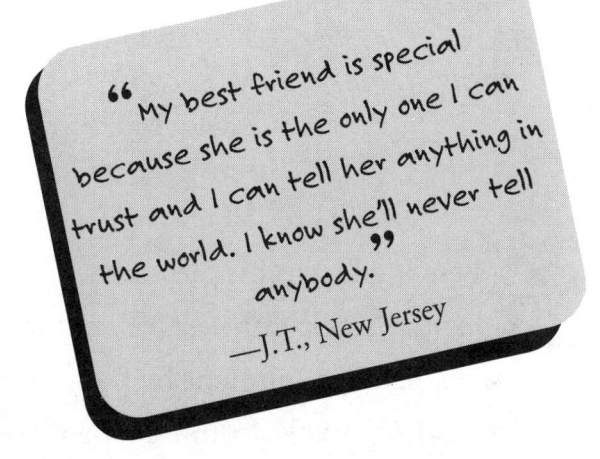

> "My best friend is special because she is the only one I can trust and I can tell her anything in the world. I know she'll never tell anybody."
> —J.T., New Jersey

> "We've always been like sisters. Ever since kindergarten, when I spotted her in these overalls."
> —Katie Holmes, actress, talking about her best friend, Meghann

# CHAPTER 1

# WHAT FRIENDSHIP IS ALL ABOUT

*Finding friends is easy. Keeping them is more difficult.*
—Author Unknown

A best friendship can be one of the most rewarding experiences a girl ever has, but it takes loyalty, honesty, and a real commitment by both of you to make a good friendship work. In this chapter, you and your buds will find helpful hints and tips for strengthening your friendships and making them better than ever.

## BE A BETTER BUDDY

Are you the best friend you can be? Take the quick quiz on the following page and find out. All you have to do is grab a sheet of paper and write down the numbers 1 through 10. Read each question, then put a "T" if the statement is true or an "F" if it's false beside the appropriate number on your paper.

1. I always keep my best friend's secrets.
2. My best friend isn't perfect, but that doesn't change how much I care about her.
3. I never bail on plans with my best friend, even if I'm invited at the last minute to a supercool party.
4. We fight, but then we're over it.
5. I give my best friend advice without sounding like a mom.
6. No matter what we're doing, I always have fun with my best friend.
7. My best friend and I get along great because we can be ourselves around each other.
8. Even when we don't agree, I respect my best friend's opinions.
9. I never try to grab attention from my best friend.
10. I never, ever talk about my best friend behind her back.

# How to Score:

Give yourself one point for every answer you marked true. Figure out your "super-friend" status using this rating system:
• 8–10 points: You're a true friend, and your best friend probably knows it. • 5–7 points: You could be a bit more sensitive, but you have potential. • 0–4 points: Yikes! It's time for you to learn about being a friend. Turn the page.

# TERRIFIC TRAITS

You've heard it before: To *have* a friend, you must *be* a friend. But what does that really mean? For starters, it means putting the Golden Rule into practice and treating others the way you want to be treated.

> "Friends can tell me, 'You're full of it,' and I have to listen."
> —Cher, singer and actress

Here are the traits every good friend has or should try to have:

- ★ Be a good listener.
- ★ Be accepting.
- ★ Be nice.
- ★ Be trustworthy.

If you fit all of the above, you'll make friends and keep them.

# ON BEING YOURSELF

There's only one you, and that's what makes you special! You may have all the traits of a perfect friend, but when you try to act like someone you're not, you won't feel good about yourself. What's worse, you'll probably attract friends who aren't right for you.

When you're with your best friend, you know you don't have to pretend to be anyone else—you can just be yourself. Best friends should be able to watch each other cry, share each other's laughter, and act incredibly silly. Once you develop a strong friendship with someone special, that relationship can work like magic to help you feel okay about what kind of a person you are. So, pick your friends carefully and keep in mind that a best buddy should be able to:

- ☆ Listen to anything you tell her without making fun of you.
- ☆ Give you a shoulder to cry on.
- ☆ Give advice when needed, *without* criticizing.
- ☆ Not be judgmental.

## Famous Friendships from Movies

It's Saturday night. Your best friends are coming over for a slumber party. Why not have a movie marathon that really matters? Show your favorite films that feature great friendships! Here are some of the best.

Wayne (Mike Myers) and Garth (Dana Carvey) in *Wayne's World*, 1992

Huck Finn (Elijah Wood) and Jim (Robbie Coltrane) in *The Adventures of Huckleberry Finn*, 1993

Mary (Kate Maberly), Colin (Heydon Prowse), and Dickon (Andrew Knott) in *The Secret Garden*, 1993

Jesse (Jason James Richter) and Willy in *Free Willy*, 1993

E.T. and Elliot (Henry Thomas) in *E.T.*, 1982

C. C. Bloom (Bette Midler) and Hilary Whitney (Barbara Hershey) in *Beaches*, 1988

M'Lynn (Sally Field), Truvy (Dolly Parton), Ouiser (Shirley MacLaine), Annelle Cici (Daryl Hannah), Claree (Olympia Dukakis), and Shelby (Julia Roberts) in *Steel Magnolias*, 1989

Ariel and Flounder in *The Little Mermaid*, 1989

Vada (Anna Chlumsky) and Thomas James (Macaulay Culkin) in *My Girl*, 1991

Roberta (Christina Ricci, Rosie O'Donnell), Teeny (Thora Birch, Melanie Griffith), Samantha (Gaby Hoffman, Demi Moore), and Chrissy (Ashleigh Aston Moore, Rita Wilson) in *Now and Then*, 1995

> "It is one of the blessings of old friends that you can afford to be stupid with them."
> —Ralph Waldo Emerson, teacher and author

# 20 FRIENDSHIP DOs AND DON'Ts

Ever wonder how some girls get to be so popular and have tons of pals—maybe even several best friends? It all starts with liking yourself and respecting others. Here are some hints for developing first-rate friendships.

1. **Do** choose your friends carefully.

2. **Do** learn to make the first move. Maybe you'll want to call to say hello during summer vacation or be the one to apologize after a fight. Don't always wait for someone else to take action.

3. **Do** learn how to accept compliments. If someone pays you a compliment, don't blow it off. Just smile and say, "Thank you." Don't put yourself down. Pals will get tired of having to reassure you.

4. **Do** pump up your friends. Everyone likes to hear something good about themselves. Let your friends know what's special about them.

5. **Don't** tease friends. It's never any fun to be the brunt of someone's joke. Be kind.

6. **Do** be true to yourself. Be honest about how you feel about things. Don't look to others to confirm your opinions or tell you how you should think.

7. **Do** be someone others can count on. If you say you're going to be somewhere at a certain time, be there. Flaky friends are never lasting friends.

8. **Don't** brag about things or be a show-off. Let others notice what's special about you.

9. **Don't** blame your friends when things go wrong for you. If someone gets an A on a book report and you don't, realize the problem isn't her. Maybe next time you can work together.

10. **Do** spend time apart. It's great to have a best friend, but hanging out with other people sometimes makes life more interesting and might even keep your friendship stronger. If you're too needy, your friend may say, "See ya."

11. **Do** remember ways to make your friendship special. You might want to decorate her bedroom for her birthday or make an all-out effort to buy her just the right holiday gift. Make sure she knows how much she means to you.

12. **Don't** go after her crush. Once she tells you who she's crushing on, he's off-limits to you.

13. **Don't** blab her secrets or talk about her to others. Nobody wants a friend who's two-faced or has a big mouth.

14. **Don't** be bossy. All relationships are about compromise. If she always wants to ice-skate and you prefer bowling, figure out a way both of you can be happy. A good friend knows she can't always have it her way.

15. **Don't** get mad and quit talking. Even the closest friends fight. Tell your friend what's bugging you. She can't change without knowing what the problem is.

16. **Do** be sensitive to her needs. It doesn't matter if she just had a fight with her sister or was caught passing a note in class—let her know you're there for her.

17. **Don't** dump your friends for someone new. It's okay to develop other friendships, but keep working on the ones you have.

18. **Don't** use your friends. Frequently asking to borrow clothes, money, homework assignments, etc., can add up to a big fight.

19. **Don't** be jealous. Whether she has better grades, a fabulous haircut, or a killer serve in volleyball, let her have her turn to shine.

20. **Do** realize that friendships change. As times goes by, you may grow apart. If this happens, deal with it—by talking it out and being totally honest. If it's time to rethink the friendship, do it as gently as possible.

# HOW DOES YOUR FRIENDSHIP RATE?

If you're wondering how your friendship scores, check out these revealing signs.

## Your Friendship Is for Real If:

- ☺ You have a lot of interests in common.
- ☺ You enjoy each other's company most of the time.
- ☺ She calls you often and has your number on her speed dial.
- ☺ She has you on her "buddy list" so she'll know when you're on-line.
- ☺ She invites you to spend the night almost every weekend.
- ☺ She saves you a seat next to her on the bus or at lunch.

## You Could Be Headed for a Friendship Failure If:

- ☹ She ignores you.
- ☹ You're the one who always calls her.
- ☹ She cancels plans at the last minute.
- ☹ When you ask her to do something, she is usually busy.
- ☹ She talks about you behind your back.
- ☹ She only calls you when she needs something or when everyone else is busy.

CHAPTER

## 2

# FRIENDSHIP CHALLENGES

*Friendship is a plant that one must water often.*
—German Proverb

Every friendship is special. But sometimes, special circumstances make some friendships a little more challenging than others. If your best friend is moving, you're friends with a boy, or your threesome is getting kind of tiresome, this chapter's for you. Read on.

## LONG-DISTANCE FRIENDSHIPS

You've got the greatest best friend in the world, and one day she tells you she's moving away. What should you do?

- A  Hire terrorists to hijack the moving truck and bring her back.
- B  Pack yourself in a box and move with her.
- C  Dry your eyes and read the following tips on keeping faraway friendships going.

Letter C, of course! Grab a hankie and read on!

# GAMES GIRLS PLAY

Whether your best friend lives two thousand miles away or just across town, spice up the connection between you and your pal by sending her some creative correspondence!

*The Puzzle Letter:* Write your friend a one-page letter on plain white paper. (Be sure to include lots of exciting information and juicy news!) When you're done writing, glue the letter to a sheet of cardboard that's the same size as your paper. Wait two hours for the glue to dry, then cut the cardboard into tiny puzzle pieces. Put all the puzzle pieces into a small box and ship it to your pal with T.L.C. (that's Tender Loving Care). She'll have a blast figuring out the mangled message!

*Mystery Mail:* On a sheet of plain white or colored paper, write your friend a message using a personalized secret code. Create a symbol for every letter of the alphabet and use the symbols to state your message. For instance, ✿ ○✺✹✹ ⚬⚬ ♡ ✸ can translate into "I miss you." Be sure to include a copy of the code key so that she can decipher the special saying and send back a note to you.

*Group Greeting:* Take a snapshot of yourself with some of your mutual friends. Tape it to a sheet of sturdy paper and have the whole group write special notes to your buddy and sign their names. Your long-distance friend will love you for it.

*Crossword Connection:* Create a crossword puzzle using special moments or favorite memories as your clues. (For instance: 2 Down—Our favorite food to pig out on; 9 Across—The place we love to spend time.) Refer to the crossword puzzle in your newspaper if you need an example.

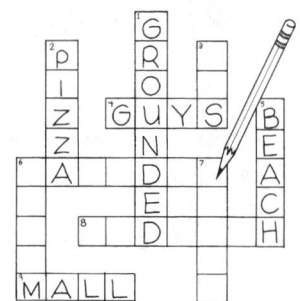

## FARAWAY FRIEND TESTIMONIALS

If you or your friend has moved away, whether it's across the country or to the other side of town, you don't have to grow apart. Keep your friendship close with these tips:

Make a promise to keep in touch and stick to it. Before you or she leaves town, agree on how to stay connected. Maybe you can call or write to her every other Saturday, and she can call or write to you twice a month, too.

Listen to what some girls have to say about their long-distance friendships:

> *I was crushed when Lisa told me her dad got transferred out of state. I thought I'd never be able to smile again! But boy, was I wrong. We're closer than ever before because we write letters and call every week. This summer, my parents are even letting me visit her for two weeks!*
> —Kelsey, 12

> *Brittany and I met in the fifth grade and she moved away a year later. We've been best friends for three years now. Sure, I've made other friends, but my connection with her is special in spite of the distance. I pour my deepest secrets out to her in letters. Sometimes that's easier than talking face-to-face!*
> —Ginny, 13

*Whenever I'm feeling bummed out or sad, I write a long letter to my best friend in Michigan. She always writes me back and says just the right thing. We'll be best buddies forever . . . I just know it.*

—Marie, 10

# BEST FRIENDS WITH A . . . BOY?

Why would a girl want to be best friends with a boy? Probably because he can give her a whole different view on all kinds of situations. And some girls feel more comfortable hanging around guys than girls.

> "He is not my boyfriend! He's my friend, and I only surround myself with people I find intellectually stimulating!"
> —Vada (Anna Chlumsky), from the film *My Girl*

If you want to strengthen the friendship between you and a guy, or if you already have a boy buddy, here are a few tips:

*1. Be prepared to gain a new perspective.* Unless you've been hanging around boys all your life, you're probably not accustomed to their ways! Your friend may be able to introduce you to new sports, games, places, and ideas. Be open to his suggestions. Then, see if he'll try some of your favorite pastimes.

*2. Don't feel that you have to explain to the whole world that the two of you are "only friends."* In time, others will see that your relationship is based on friendship and nothing else. By making an issue out of it, you may be creating a problem where one doesn't exist.

*3. Ask his advice and give some, too!* It can be great to learn how a boy thinks, and he'll probably be glad that you trust him enough to ask for his opinions. Help him out, too, by offering your own ideas and suggestions.

**4. Follow the same rules in your boy/girl friendships that you do in your other friendships.** Listen to him, and be accepting, encouraging, and honest.

Remember, to have a friend, you must be a friend—even when that friend's a *he*!

## WHEN THREE'S COMPANY

Wouldn't it be great if all of your friends always got along whenever you got together? Well, the truth is, that isn't likely. Not everyone's going to get along all of the time, no matter how much you want them to or how hard you try to keep things together.

And if your group is a threesome, it can be a real challenge to keep the peace. The good news is that you have two special people to turn to for support and good times. The bad news is that one friend can feel left out.

If you've got a three-way connection that needs some help, here are some things to think about.

When you are all together as a trio, talk things over. Ignoring the problem won't make it go away. Maybe one of you doesn't realize how you're coming across.

Try to have a sense of humor about what's happened. Can the three of you find anything funny about the situation?

Remember to make your plans according to how many of you there will be. Some activities are great with three participants, like watching videos or going bowling. But you may want to think twice before heading to an amusement park where some rides hold only two passengers per car.

If you're the one in your group who feels left out, try to get together with each of your other two friends separately from time to time. That way, you'll establish your own strong relationships one on one.

Don't single out one person in the group and treat them better than the other person. Be an equally good friend to both of your buds, and make sure they do the same. Remind both of your friends that each of you is special for a different reason. That's what makes your trio so terrific!

When you do get together as a threesome, here are a few awesome activities to do together. You'll have so much fun and you'll keep so busy, your friendship can't help but stay on track.

*1. Have a treasure hunt.* One person puts together a series of clues for her two best friends that leads them on a hunt around the neighborhood. When the two "hunters" reach their last clue, they win a prize—like tickets to a movie—for three, of course.

*2. Go on a picnic.* Get together and work as a group to prepare a "to go" menu. Then pack up everything and take it somewhere fun.

*3. Put on a play.* Two people can be the actors, and the third can be the director and video-camera operator. Or, all three friends can make up a skit to perform for family, other buddies, or just a few cherished stuffed animals!

*4. Have a study session.* If two heads are better than one, then three heads must be the best! (And study breaks will be triple the fun!)

*5. Get everyone together for a manicure.* Call ahead to a nail salon and book an appointment for your threesome. Meet at someone's house ahead of time and bring your favorite nail polishes. Have fun deciding what polish colors to wear.

*6. Create your own "Best Friends Forever" Web page.* It's a fun project—your threesome can gather around the computer monitor together and make this a group effort. You can check out a site like Angelfire.com or Geocities.com for helpful how-tos. Or you can use a search engine like Altavista and see what kind of information is available. AOL members can type in a keyword to get to a Web page where they'll find some tips. If you don't think you're computer savvy enough to do this, try creating a friendship newsletter.

**7. Try baking or cooking together.** Whip up a batch of chocolate chip pancakes for breakfast, or try out one of your mom's favorite cookie recipes. Creating something special is a perfect recipe for fun.

**8. Get your friends together and write letters to each other.** Be sure to include lots of details about your friendship. Write about what you like to do together, your favorite memories, what you're looking forward to, etc. Include info on your favorite band, movie, TV show, magazine, or book. Then address and stamp the envelopes. Ask one of your moms to keep the letters for one year, then mail them out. It'll be fun to get together to see what you wrote and look back on what you were doing.

Look in chapter 5 for loads of other entertaining activities, regardless of the number of friends involved—a pair, a quartet, even a dozen!

CHAPTER

# 3

# RESOLVING PAL PROBLEMS

*Real friends are those who, when you've made a fool of yourself, don't feel that you've done a permanent job.*
—Author Unknown

You feel so lucky! You know you have the best friend anyone could ever ask for. She's more fun than anyone else you know, and she's always there for you. She laughs at your dumb jokes and tells you you're great even when you don't feel you are. She even puts up with you when you're being a brat! So, what happens when a disagreement turns into a big blowup? Do you walk away, or hang tough and try to work through the problem?

> "The quickest way to spoil a friendship is to wake somebody up in the morning before he is ready."
> —E. B. White, *Charlotte's Web*

# FIGHTING FAIR WITH YOUR BEST FRIEND

Let's face it. The two of you won't always agree on everything all the time. If you haven't already had a war with your best friend, you will. And that's okay! It's human nature to disagree, and in the end, you may even strengthen your friendship. Here's what to do when a fight breaks out:

*1. Tell her what she did that upset you.* If you're angry because she bailed out on seeing a movie at the very last minute, let her know. Don't keep it inside.

> ✗ **Don't say (if you're seething inside):** "Oh, I'm fine. No, really. It's only the fourth time you broke our movie date in a week. But I'm fine."

> ✓ **Say:** "I can't believe you flaked. I was counting on seeing that show with you. What happened?"

*2. Focus on the actions of your friend rather than your friend, personally.* Be clear about the fact that you're unhappy with her behavior and not her as a person. Instead of criticizing her and calling her names, concentrate on how her actions made you feel.

> ✗ **Don't say:** "I can't believe how unfair you are . . . not to mention inconsiderate and mean. You know how much I wanted to see that movie!"

> ✓ **Say:** "When you didn't go, it hurt my feelings."

*3. Focus your feelings on specifics rather than making generalizations.* Using words like "always" and "never" will only put her on the defensive and she'll be tempted to argue with you.

> ✗ **Don't say:** "You know, you're *always* blowing me off! You *never* follow through with our plans."

> ✓ **Say:** "I was really bummed that you didn't show up."

**4. Let her know how her actions made you feel, but don't judge her motives.** When you discuss the event that has you upset, don't try and figure out why she hurt you. If you do, she'll probably be so busy defending herself that you'll never resolve the conflict.

✗ **Don't say:** "I know you did this on purpose just because you thought I wouldn't get mad. You're always dumping on me!"

✓ **Say:** "Seeing that movie was really important to me! I thought you wanted to see it, too."

**5. Put your energies toward fixing the friendship rather than "winning" an argument.** The goal of the argument should be resolving conflict and maintaining your best friendship. Don't try to "win" the fight by offering low blows or criticisms. Words said in anger can really hurt a friendship. Focus on reaching a mutual understanding so that you don't get hurt in the same way again.

✗ **Don't say:** "Everybody is getting mad at you because you're so unreliable. You're lucky I'm your friend!"

✓ **Say:** "I really want us to stay close, but we need to make sure these things don't keep happening."

Knowing how to fight right can save your friendship—and make it better.

# WHEN A FRIEND BETRAYS YOU

A best friend may betray you so badly that you simply can't (or won't) forgive her, even over a period of weeks. Maybe she spread a hurtful rumor about you. Or she told all of your classmates a secret that you had made her *promise* not to tell anyone. Only you can weigh all of the facts and decide for yourself if you're willing to continue the friendship.

But before you end the friendship, you may want to examine your own best-friend behavior. Did you do something to trigger her betrayal? Perhaps the only way to know for sure is to have a heart-to-heart talk with her. Ask yourself how you'd feel if you lost her as a friend. Do you still value her friendship enough to forgive her for what she did? If so, talk to her right away. Come up with a few ways to keep your friendship together.

If you feel there's no way to resolve things right now, you still need to take action. Talk to your friend and let her know exactly how you feel. Explain why you're hurt and why you feel the need to back off from the friendship. Then, take some time out and spend several days or even weeks apart. During this time, you should look closely at how you and your friend treat each other. This separation might be good for both of you, since the time apart will allow you to think about what happened and consider how important your friendship is. All friendships have problems. The goal is to make sure you know how to fight fair when problems arise.

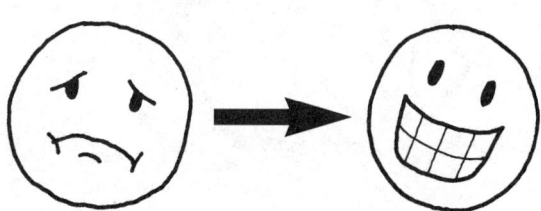

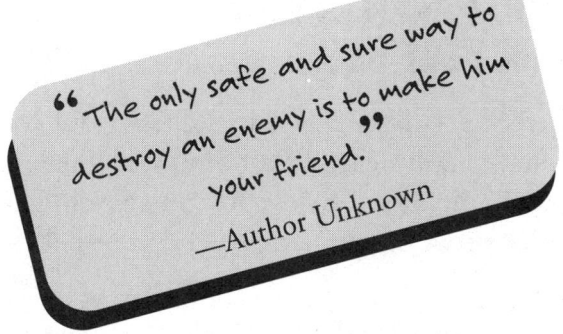

"The only safe and sure way to destroy an enemy is to make him your friend."
—Author Unknown

# 4 Quick and Easy Ways to Turn an Enemy into a Friend

If you want to patch things up, use one or more of the tips below to turn a foe back into a friend!

1. Make peace. Take the first step toward a truce by offering your apologies. Be willing to admit, "I was wrong and I'm sorry."

2. Forgive her. You can't become friends again until you forgive her—but you have to mean it!

3. Practice being completely truthful with your feelings. If you lie to her, you are saying either that you don't care enough about her to be truthful, or that you don't trust the friendship enough to confide in her.

4. Kill her with kindness. Do something sweet and sincere for her and she won't stay mad for long!

# WHEN YOU PARENTS DON'T LIKE YOUR BEST BUD

You're supertight with your best friend, but your parents think she's the female equivalent of Bart Simpson! Take steps to smooth out the situation. Below are some useful guidelines for making peace between your parents and your pal.

- Find out why your parents don't like your friend. Listen with an open mind and try not to get angry. Perhaps they know something about your friend that you don't. Chances are, your parents are just concerned about you, and for some reason they believe your best friend isn't a positive influence.

- If you sincerely believe that your friend is worth keeping and that she's good for you, write a letter to your parents explaining all the things you like about your friend. Her good qualities are bound to impress them. (If not, maybe you need to really think about why your parents feel the way they do.)

- Show your parents that you are responsible by your consistent good behavior. Assure them that no one will *cause* you to get into trouble. Once your folks see your maturity, they'll begin trusting your selection of friends.

- Plan an activity that you, your friend, and your parents can do together. The more time you and your friend spend with Mom and Dad, the more they may see your pal's prized qualities.

# How to Make (and Keep!) a Best Friend

Ask yourself, "Would I like to be best friends with me right now?" The following exercises can help make sure that you're on the right track!

- Write down your personality traits, both good and bad. Ask yourself: Do people like me? Why or why not? Take pride in all the great things that make you *you*, and work on those qualities that need a little improvement.

- Listen in on your own conversations. Do you let your friends speak freely, or do you interrupt and give too much advice where it's not wanted?

- Try to learn more about your friends. Use your natural curiosity to find out more about them and what they like and don't like. When a friend is talking, listen attentively. If you're genuinely interested in her, she'll be interested in you, too!

- Give your friends a chance to shine. If a friend is telling a funny joke to a crowd and enjoying the attention, don't chime in with the punch line. No one wants to be overshadowed by a friend!

- Don't gossip or agree with someone who loves flapping her lips about everyone and everything! If you don't feel like defending the person who is being talked about, simply state that you feel uncomfortable with the subject and walk away.

If you treat others as you would like to be treated, you will never have to worry about whether your friends really like you. Your biggest problem will be finding enough time to spend with all your friends!

# WHEN FRIENDSHIPS FADE AWAY

Some friendships really do last forever, but others come and go. Sometimes it's mutual and the friendship just kind of drifts apart. Interests change. Someone moves. You go to different schools.

It's great when both parties decide to end a friendship at the same time, but that doesn't always happen. When the decision is one-sided, someone is left feeling sad and angry.

If this happens to you, remember it's not the end of the world, though it may seem like it. Try to remind yourself that it's natural to outgrow some friendships. It doesn't mean that anyone has done anything wrong or that one of you is mean and uncaring.

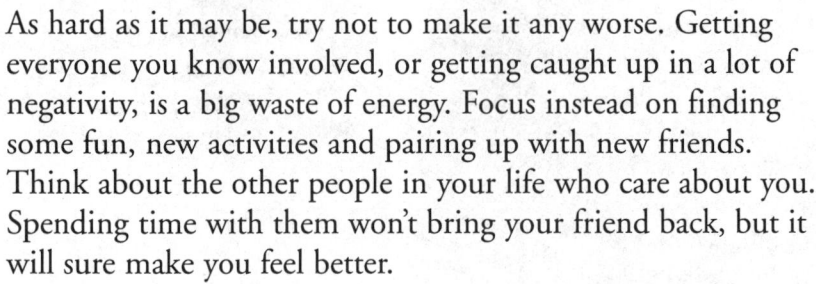

As hard as it may be, try not to make it any worse. Getting everyone you know involved, or getting caught up in a lot of negativity, is a big waste of energy. Focus instead on finding some fun, new activities and pairing up with new friends. Think about the other people in your life who care about you. Spending time with them won't bring your friend back, but it will sure make you feel better.

Ask yourself what you learned from this situation that might help you with future friendships. Could you have been a better friend? Did you spend too much time with just one friend at the expense of other relationships?

Remember, your friend has moved on, but there are lots of new friendships waiting to find you.

# FIX THOSE FRIENDSHIPS

Here's some advice on handling those friendship problems that everyone has now and then.

**Q** *I just moved to another state and I'm miserable! I've always gone to school with the same kids. I was popular, had lots of friends, and was a good student. I want to make friends here, but I don't know how. Help!*

—L.H., San Diego, California

**A** Starting over at a new school can be tough. But since you were well liked at your old school, had many friends, and made good grades, there's no reason that you won't be accepted in your new school, too. All the qualities that made you a valued member of your old group are the same ones that will help you now. Give yourself lots of opportunities to get involved with different groups of people . . . and don't forget to smile and be friendly.

**Q** *My best friend has been ganging up with another friend and putting me down. When I complain, they say, "We were just kidding," or "Don't be so sensitive." I'm sick of taking their criticisms. What should I do?*

—A.P., Winona, Minnesota

**A** Your pals aren't playing fair! When you defend yourself, they put the blame back on you by saying you're too sensitive. Tell them how you feel. If they don't seem willing to listen, involve yourself in activities with other people. Once your friends see that you won't stand for their put-downs, they should start treating you better. If they don't, find friends who will.

**Q.** *I'm known as the person everyone can trust and count on. My best friend is always telling me her problems and asking for advice. Even though I love to listen and help, I'm so busy figuring out her life that I don't have time for mine! What should I do?*

—L.C., Idaho Falls, Idaho

**A.** Your role as listener and advice-giver is certainly an admirable one, but as you've discovered, it can become one-sided. Start by approaching your friend with a problem of your own. She'll probably be glad that she can help you out in return. After all, friendship is a two-way street.

**Q.** *My best friend told me she got an A on a paper right after I showed her that I got an A. Then, the assignment fell out of her notebook and I saw a huge red C written on it. Why would she lie to me? It makes me wonder if she lies about other things, too.*

—T.H., Loveland, Colorado

**A.** There could be many reasons why your friend fibbed about her grade, but most likely she was embarrassed about the C. Maybe she is having a difficult time in school. Or she may feel threatened by you and other students. The important thing now is to talk about it. Offer to help her study next time. Let her know that you'll be her best friend no matter what grade she gets. Make sure you tell her how important honesty is to your friendship, too.

**Q.** *My best friend of five years just transferred to a private school. Lately, she's become stuck-up and very distant. She even told me that I needed to go on a diet and that my hair looked terrible! She's always saying how popular she is at her new school and how everyone likes her. I feel bad whenever we're together. What can I do?*

—W.V., Portland, Oregon

**A** Maybe your friend is actually feeling insecure with her new surroundings and is bragging to you in order to build up her ego. Maybe she thinks that by putting you down, she'll build herself up. That doesn't mean that you have to stand for it. Friends are supposed to make you feel better about yourself, not worse. Let her know that her behavior is making you feel awful, and unless she stops, you're not going to hang around her for a while. She'll either get a clue and change her behavior, or leave you free to enjoy new friends who will help you feel good about yourself.

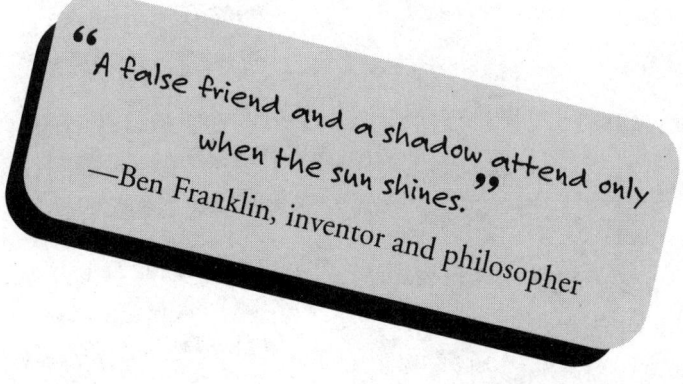

"A false friend and a shadow attend only when the sun shines."
—Ben Franklin, inventor and philosopher

> "My best friend is the best thing that has ever happened to me. She is there for me every time I need her. She understands me as if she is me. Her friendship means everything to me."
>
> —J.J., Wisconsin

## A History of Famous TV Friendships

In TV land, friendships are built, destroyed, then put back together again—all in a thirty-minute time slot. Here are some of the best TV-made friendships in television history, many of which you can catch either on prime time or a syndicated station.

Blossom (Mayim Bialik) and Six (Jenna Von Oy) in *Blossom*

Lois (Terri Hatcher) and Clark (Dean Cain) in *Lois & Clark: The New Adventures of Superman*

Tia (Tia Mowry) and Tamara (Tamara Mowry) in *Sister, Sister*

Lucy (Lucille Ball) and Ethel (Vivian Vance) in *I Love Lucy*

Mary (Mary Tyler Moore) and Rhoda (Valerie Harper) in *The Mary Tyler Moore Show*

Laverne (Penny Marshall) and Shirley (Cindy Williams) in *Laverne & Shirley*

Kelly (Jennie Garth) and Donna (Tori Spelling) in *Beverly Hills, 90210*

Buffy (Sarah Michelle Gellar) and Willow (Alyson Hannigan) in *Buffy the Vampire Slayer*

Topanga (Danielle Fishel) and Angela (Trina McGee-Davis) in *Boy Meets World*

# CHAPTER 4

# GIFTS AND CRAFTS FOR 4-EVER FRIENDS

*This is my advice. Give a glittering scale to each of the other fish. You will no longer be the most beautiful fish in the sea, but you will discover how to be happy.*
—Marcus Pfister, *The Rainbow Fish*

Your friend spends a whole weekend helping you with your chores, and then she lets you cry on her shoulder over not making the school's soccer team. Maybe the two of you have just made up after a huge fight. Or, you just want to do something extra-special for her birthday or the holidays. What can you do to show that you care? Here are some creative and memorable gifts you can make yourself.

> "A friend is a present which you give yourself."
> —Robert Louis Stevenson, author

# THE BIRTHDAY TREE

You don't need a green thumb to give this friendship plant—just a little thoughtfulness and some imagination!

## You Need:

- small tree or large plant
- wrapping paper, ribbon
- tape
- friendship mementos (pictures, ticket stubs, etc.)

## What to Do:

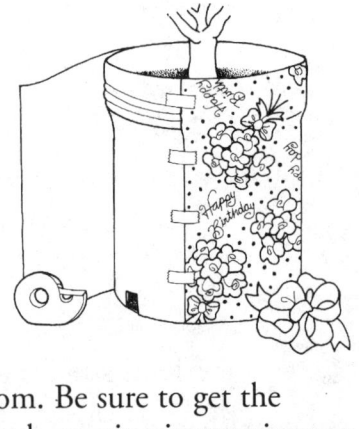

1. About a week before your friend's birthday, go to the nursery or garden center and look at the miniature trees (the kind that grow in pots) or the flowering plants. Buy an especially beautiful one that is blooming or just about to bloom. Be sure to get the nursery to write down the care and watering instructions so you can include them with your gift.

2. To give your gift some birthday flair, tape colorful wrapping paper around the pot and add a cute bow. Hang a card from one of the limbs. You can hang other mementos as well, such as old snapshots, secret notes, and dried flowers.

3. When you present your friend with the special gift, don't forget to point out to her that the tree will bloom right around her birthday every year!

# 10 Reasons to Give a Gift to a Friend

1. **To say thanks:** She helped you study for a big test and you both aced it.

2. **To help her through a change:** She's just moved into a new house or she just found out she has to share her bedroom with her sister.

3. **To celebrate a fun event:** The two of you just had a great time together, such as at a concert, on a bike ride, or on a special trip.

4. **Because you remember:** While shopping one day, you notice how much she admires something, so you take the time to buy or make it for her.

5. **To celebrate a job well done:** She made the school volleyball team, or has just been elected president of her class.

6. **To cheer her up:** Everybody has a bad day now and then. A small gift from a special best friend can really brighten up her day.

7. **To pass it on:** You have a sweater or other item that you don't like but she has always loved. Give it to her, as long as it's okay with Mom or Dad.

8. **To solve a double dilemma:** If you receive a gift of something you already have, give the duplicate to your friend.

9. **To say you're sorry:** Maybe it wasn't even a fight, but there was a misunderstanding. Besides apologizing, a small gift can go a long way toward patching things up again.

10. **Just because:** No special reason—you just want to give your friend a gift she'll never forget.

## DOUBLE-THE-FUN EARRINGS

Are you short on time, but you want the world to know you're best friends? This is a gift you'll love as much as she will.

### You Need:
- small box
- pretty ribbon
- two pairs of inexpensive earrings that look good together

### What to Do:

1. Go shopping for two pairs of inexpensive earrings that complement each other, such as two different-colored pairs that represent your school colors, or a pair of earrings in her favorite color and a pair in your favorite color. You can even mix ideas. If she likes dogs and you like cats, find one pair of earrings with dogs and another pair with cats.

2. Now do a switcheroo! Put one earring from one set and one earring from the other set into a small box. Wrap it up with a ribbon.

3. Give it to your best friend with a note. You keep the other earrings! Now you and your friend can wear your pairs of earrings together to show everyone you two are a perfect match.

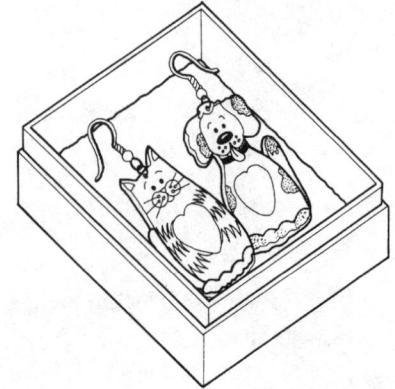

# Famous Friendship Songs

Do you have a friend who's been feeling a little down? Pop one of these tunes into your CD player or request one on your favorite radio station and dedicate it to your blue buddy—then watch her blues float away!

"That's What Friends Are For," Dionne Warwick

"You're My Best Friend," Queen

"Me and My Friends," Red Hot Chili Peppers

"Anytime You Need a Friend," Mariah Carey

"You've Got a Friend in Me," Randy Newman

"Friends Are Friends Forever," Michael W. Smith

"I'll Be There For You" (theme song from the TV show *Friends*), the Rembrandts

"Find Yourself a Friend," Hammer

"I Could Have Been Your Best Friend," Bonnie Raitt

"He's My Best Friend," Jellyfish

"I Will Be Your Friend," Sade

"If You Really Want to Be My Friend," Rolling Stones

"Whenever I Call You Friend," Kenny Loggins

"You've Got a Friend," James Taylor

## FRIENDSHIP PHOTO CALENDAR

You've been best friends for as long as you can remember, and you want to give her a gift that will last all year. Whip up a whole bunch of wonderful memories that your friend can enjoy for 365 days and then treasure as a keepsake for years to come.

### You Need:

- inexpensive month-by-month calendar, with an image above each month
- white glue
- scissors
- memorabilia, including photos of you and your best friend from throughout the year
- construction paper, various colors
- old magazines and newspapers
- wax paper
- colored pens

### What to Do:

1. Gather memorabilia that represents your special friendship, such as pictures, ticket stubs, napkins, flowers, or even cutouts from magazines that show the types of things your best friend loves to do.

2. Separate these things into twelve piles to represent the months of the year. You may want to give each month a different theme, such as memorabilia of summer activities in July, preparing for school in August, and colorful fall pictures in September.

**3.** Open the calendar so that the month of January shows. Lay the pictures and cutouts you've designated for January over the calendar photograph, overlapping them until the calendar image is completely covered. If there are any open spaces, simply cover them up with small pieces of colored construction paper. Now glue these cutouts into place. As you create each collage, place a piece of wax paper on top of it. Then, as you turn the calendar pages, they will stay separated, and if any glue seeps out, your pages won't stick together. Leave the wax paper in place overnight to dry.

**4.** When the glue has dried, remove the wax paper. Go through the calendar and mark off special days, such as her birthday, friends' birthdays, the first and last days of school, holidays, and the best concerts coming to town.

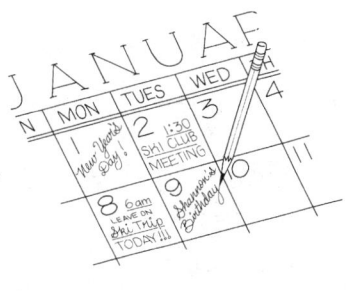

**5.** Finally, decorate the front and back covers of the calendar. You may want to use a special photograph of you and your best friend together. Have a family member take one picture of the two of you facing the camera for the front cover, and a second shot of you and your friend with your backs to the camera for the back of the calendar. Don't tell your friend what the pictures are for. Then, when she receives her personalized calendar, she'll be surprised beyond belief!

# BIRTHDAY COLLAGE

Create a collage that celebrates your friend's birthday and her own special gifts. Think up one word for every year. If she's turning ten, call it 10 Reasons You're Awesome. Use words like "friendly," "fun," "athletic," "loyal," "smart," "loving," "funny," etc. Then find pictures to illustrate the words. You might even put a big picture of her right in the middle of your project.

## You Need:

- large piece of poster board at least 14" x 24"
- crayons, markers, and paints in various colors
- paintbrush
- scissors
- glue
- construction paper
- glitter
- pictures to illustrate the words you've chosen to describe your friend—maybe even a picture of her

## What to Do:

1. Take some of the bigger pictures and trim them into different shapes. Then write your heading on the poster board.

2. Place the items on the cardboard one by one. You might want to arrange them loosely in some sort of design first, then glue them down. Write your descriptive words close to the corresponding picture, or write the words on construction paper cut into shapes, then glue into place.

3. Now add artistic flair to your collage by swishing strokes of paint here and there, outlining some of the items in crayon or marker, using glue and glitter to form decorative lines, etc.

# FRIENDSHIP BOX

**ADULT SUPERVISION RECOMMENDED**

This box is the perfect place for storing ticket stubs, private notes, pictures, and anything else your friend holds near and dear to her heart!

## You Need:

- empty shoe box with lid
- colorful wrapping paper, pages from your favorite magazine, and photos of your best buddy
- scissors
- glue
- shellac
- paintbrush

## What to Do:

1. Begin by cutting squares and rectangles of various sizes from wrapping paper and magazine pages. Cut enough to cover the outside of both the lid and the box.

2. Attach the lid to the box by cutting the two back corners of the lid up the corner creases. Spread glue across the entire lip of the lid, from one cut corner to the other. Press it firmly to the shoe box. Now you should be able to lift the lid and close it like a jewelry box.

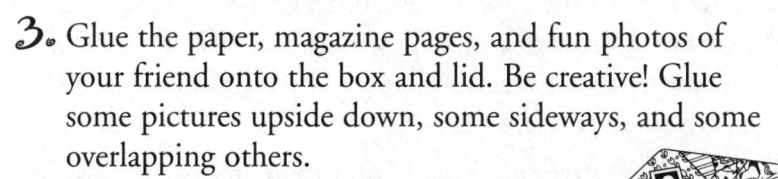

3. Glue the paper, magazine pages, and fun photos of your friend onto the box and lid. Be creative! Glue some pictures upside down, some sideways, and some overlapping others.

4. When the entire box and lid are covered, paint the box with shellac and let it dry completely. Give your treasure to a true friend or make one for yourself.

# MAKIN' MEMORIES "NOTE"BOOK
**ADULT SUPERVISION RECOMMENDED**

Any pal will flip over this handmade book—a special spot for both of you to scribble down your secret thoughts, or a place to write those special notes you send back and forth to each other.

## You Need:
- two pieces of 7" x 10" gray construction paper
- rubber cement
- scissors
- two pieces of heavy 6" x 9" cardboard
- decorative piece of floral paper (like wrapping paper)
- hole punch
- ruler
- pencil
- eraser
- stack of 6" x 9" writing paper
- 15" piece of decorative string or twine

## What to Do:

1. Spread the rubber cement evenly on the back of one of the pieces of construction paper, then apply a piece of the 6" x 9" cardboard to the center of the paper. Wrap the ½" border of the paper around the sides so that the cardboard front and sides are completely covered. You may have to apply more rubber cement to get the corners to stay down. Repeat with the second piece of cardboard and construction paper. These are the front and back covers of your book.

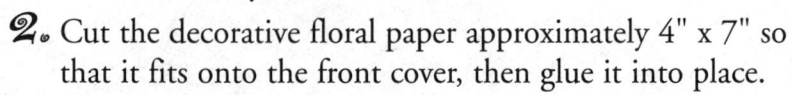

2. Cut the decorative floral paper approximately 4" x 7" so that it fits onto the front cover, then glue it into place.

3. Now it's time to punch holes in the covers. On both pieces of cardboard, measure ¾" from their left sides. With a ruler, draw a faint pencil line down the length of the book at the

¾" point. Next, measure 2" from the bottom of the cardboard and mark an X on the line. Measure 3" above that and mark another X. Finally, measure up 2" and draw an X. Do this for both the front and back covers.

4. Stack the two pieces of cardboard together with the Xs running down the left side on the front cover. Make sure that the Xs on the front cover match up exactly with the Xs on the back cover. Punch holes over all the Xs with the hole punch. Erase any visible pencil markings.

5. Place the stack of 6" x 9" paper between the two pieces of cardboard so that the left sides of the paper are even with the left sides of the covers.

6. Next, stick the pencil inside the holes in the cardboard, then draw three little circles onto the paper where you'll punch the holes. This step is tricky, since you must hold the stack of paper and cardboard completely still as you make your markings. When your markings are accurate, punch holes in the paper. If the hole punch won't go through the whole stack, punch fewer sheets at a time, but make sure all the holes are in the same location.

7. Now you are ready to loosely string together the book. Take your piece of twine and tie a double knot in the end. Starting from the back side, string the twine up through the bottom hole and come down through the next set of holes. Pull the twine back up through the top and final hole. Tie a double knot directly over the hole so that the string won't slip through. Don't string it too tightly; otherwise, the front cover may be difficult to open. You can leave the long pieces hanging or cut them off—it's up to you!

# DO-IT-YOURSELF PERSONALIZED FRAME

**ADULT SUPERVISION RECOMMENDED**

Create an original frame that can be personalized for any special friend. If you don't want to make a frame, buy a plain, inexpensive wood frame and decorate it using any of the materials mentioned in Step 6.

## You Need:

- foam-core board
- X-Acto knife
- ruler
- thick ribbon, lace, or other material
- scissors
- fabric glue
- buttons, rhinestones, or any other odds and ends
- picture of you and a friend

## What to Do:

1. First, you need to cut out your frame and its back. With an X-Acto knife and an adult's help, cut two foam-core rectangles that are an inch taller and wider than the picture you will be using. For instance, if the picture you want to use is 3½" x 5", cut two rectangles 4½" x 6".

2. On one rectangle, draw a smaller rectangle inside it that is ½" smaller all the way around. Then ask a parent to help you cut out the smaller rectangle. This is where your picture will fit.

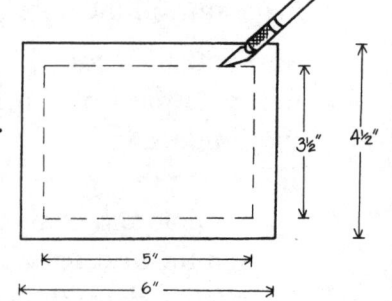

3. Now you're ready to personalize your frame! Is your friend into ballet? Grab a couple of yards of light pink netting. Is she into bright, fun colors? Find some different colors of ribbon. A nature girl? Use earthtone trims. With

the material you find, cut it into a long 1" strip. Next, start wrapping it around the rectangle with the hole. You may need to go around only once, or you may need to go around the frame a couple of times to cover all the white areas. Glue the ends into place.

4. Glue the frame (on three sides only!) onto the second rectangle. Leave one side open to stick the picture in. Let it dry.

5. As your picture frame is drying, create a small stand so your frame can rest on a table. Simply take a piece of foam-core board, about 2" x 3½", and on the 2" side, bend back ½". Then glue that ½" to the frame, making sure that the stand will rest on a flat surface.

6. If you want to add any rhinestones, shells, buttons, fake flowers, or anything else to the border of the frame, do so now using fabric glue. Let it dry.

7. Finally, put the picture of you and your friend in the frame, and you now have a gift that is sure to warm hearts for years to come!

> "You give but little when you give of your possessions. It is when you give of yourself that you truly give."
> —Kahlil Gibran, author and artist

## THREE QUICK 'N' THOUGHTFUL GIFTS FOR A FRIEND

Giving really is better than receiving, especially when you see how much your friend loves these cool homemade gifts that don't cost a lot but still show how much you're thinking of her.

### 1. Pen Pick-Me-Up

If your friend just finished a big brain-draining test, whether she aced it or bombed it, buy her a felt-tip marker in her favorite color. Glue a picture of her favorite cartoon character's head to the end of the pen that sticks up when someone is writing. Include a note with the pen that says, "Congrats, girl!" or "Better luck next time!" This thoughtful, silly gift is sure to put a smile on her face.

### 2. The Lovin' Oven

Buy a roll of packaged sugar cookie dough from the refrigerator section of the supermarket. Roll out the dough. With a simple gingerbread cookie cutter, cut cookies out in the shape of gingerbread girls. Bake them, then decorate them to look like your best friend and other classmates. "Dress" the cookies with icing, colored to imitate the latest fashions.

## 3. Tantalizing Tee

Got a friend who's down in the dumps? Give her something to get her back in the groove—a special T-shirt made just for her. Buy a T-shirt, then grab a couple of fabric markers in your friend's favorite colors and begin writing down all the words that best describe her. Is she athletic . . . brainy . . . cool . . . crafty . . . clever . . . cute . . . dramatic . . . funny? This gift should help to make her day.

## THE KEY TO GIFT GIVING

When you give something to a friend, make it an offering from your heart. Don't ever feel you must buy somebody's friendship in order to be accepted.

The time and effort you put into thinking up, planning, and creating a personal present will be appreciated more than the gift itself, and it will express the real depth and meaning of your friendship. A handmade gift says to your friend and to the world, "My best friend is one very special person!"

> "Friendship is to be purchased only by friendship."
> —Author Unknown

> "My best bud and I have been joined at the hip ever since we were introduced. She is my inspiration. She cheers me up when I am down. We have been through the good, the bad, and the ugly together. I know we will be friends forever."
> —E.B., Pennsylvania

# CHAPTER 5

# THINGS TO DO WITH YOU-KNOW-WHO!

*The most I can do for my friend is simply to be his friend.*
—Henry David Thoreau, author

One of the best ways to develop strong friendships is to spend time together. Of course, sitting around watching old reruns of *Gilligan's Island* or *The Brady Bunch* is not the most ideal pastime on which to build a friendship!

This chapter will give you some creative and fun activities that you and your friends can do together.

## THE RAINY-DAY RETREAT

*Ideal number of friends: two or four (pairs are ideal)*

Just because the weather is gloomy doesn't mean you and your best friend can't have a great time. Join the most exclusive of spas—the one in your home or hers—and give yourselves a makeover with ingredients right from your own kitchen. (The items you need to provide are in **bold type**.)

## The Evening Before:

1. Make sure it's okay with your parents to use your bedroom and one bathroom the next day for several hours.

2. Read through the retreat section below and collect all the materials you'll need for your big day.

## The Retreat!

**8 A.M.:** With your buddy, start your rainy-day retreat by working out to the hottest new **exercise video** your rental store has to offer. Or, if you have a large garage or basement, grab a **jump rope,** turn on your **favorite tunes,** and jump rope for twenty to forty minutes, depending on your level of fitness. Then do some of your favorite floor exercises (is there such a thing?), like sit-ups or leg-lifts. Stretch out your muscles for at least ten minutes when you are done.

**9:30 A.M.:** Cool down from your workout with a fresh, healthy fruit smoothie. Place 1 or 2 cups of **fresh fruit** (strawberries, bananas, and oranges work well), 1 cup of **low-fat milk,** and 1 cup of **ice** into a **blender**. Blend on high until smooth. Pour into two **tall glasses** and top with **straws**. (Depending on the number of spa enthusiasts, increase the recipe as needed.)

**10 A.M.:** Now you're ready to give each other a facial or a mask, which you can make yourself from one of the recipes at the end of this section. Always start with a clean face before applying any mask.

**10:30 A.M.:** Next, take turns taking a steamy shower and washing your hair.

**11 A.M.:** After you've dried off, put on some comfortable sweats and prepare to condition your hair. In a **small bowl,** place about ½ cup of **mayonnaise**. If you have really long hair, you may need more. Rub the mayonnaise into your damp hair.

Wrap your hair in a plastic bag or plastic wrap, then let the conditioner set for fifteen minutes.

**11:15 A.M.:** Rinse out the conditioner with warm water. Make sure you rinse really well.

**12 NOON:** Lunch break. Load up on **fresh veggies** in a big **salad**. Skip the cookies for dessert and have an **apple** instead.

**1 P.M.:** Trade off fixing each other's hair. If it's still damp and has a case of the tangles, don't use a brush. This can snap the ends and cause big-time splits. Instead, gently use a wide-tooth comb to separate the tangles. Work from the ends of your hair up to your scalp. If one of you has long, straight hair, you can braid the hair while it is still wet. Remove the braids when the hair is dry and you'll have instant waves. If you get stumped for other hairstyling ideas, check out your favorite fashion magazines.

**2:30 P.M.:** Once your hair is perfect, you can give each other a manicure. Begin by soaking your hands in a **small bowl** of warm water and a little **dishwashing soap**. Gently scrub your nails with a **nail brush,** and very gently push back the cuticles with an **orangewood stick.** Do not clip or cut them. Lightly shape the nails with an **emery board.** Pick out a dazzling shade of **nail polish**. While your nails are drying, talk about all the fantastic things you're going to do when the weather clears up.

**4 P.M.:** What a day! You've pampered yourself all day long and had lots of fun with your friend. Host another retreat the next time you and your buddy want to do something special for yourselves—there's no need to wait for rain!

## Cool Make-It-Yourself Masks

### Avocado Smoother

This mask will give any skin a silky, more soft appearance.

Mix ½ a medium-sized ripe **avocado,** 1 tablespoon of **honey,** and ¼ cup of **milk** in a **blender** or a **bowl** with a **fork** until smooth. Pin back your hair away from your face. Starting at your neck, gently massage the mixture onto your skin. Work all the way up to your forehead using upward strokes. Make sure you leave a 1" area around your eyes to protect them. Sit back, put your feet up, and relax for about twenty minutes.

Splash off the mask with warm water and then rinse with cool water. Your skin and pores will feel great.

### Egg Facials

If you prefer egg on your face, try one of these two simple beauty masks—but don't get the raw egg on your mouth!

#### #1

Mix together one fresh **egg** and enough **honey** to make a paste. Spread this mix over your face, leaving a 1" area around your eyes. Let the mask harden for fifteen to twenty minutes. Rinse with warm water to remove the mask, then splash your face with cool water to soothe your skin and tighten your pores.

#2

Have an adult help you separate the **egg whites** from the egg yolks. You will need two egg whites per girl. Beat the whites with a **fork** or an **electric beater** until frothy. Spread the whites over your face and throat, leaving a 1" area around your eyes. Let the mask dry for fifteen to twenty minutes before rinsing with cold water. The egg whites will close your pores and make your face look clean and shiny.

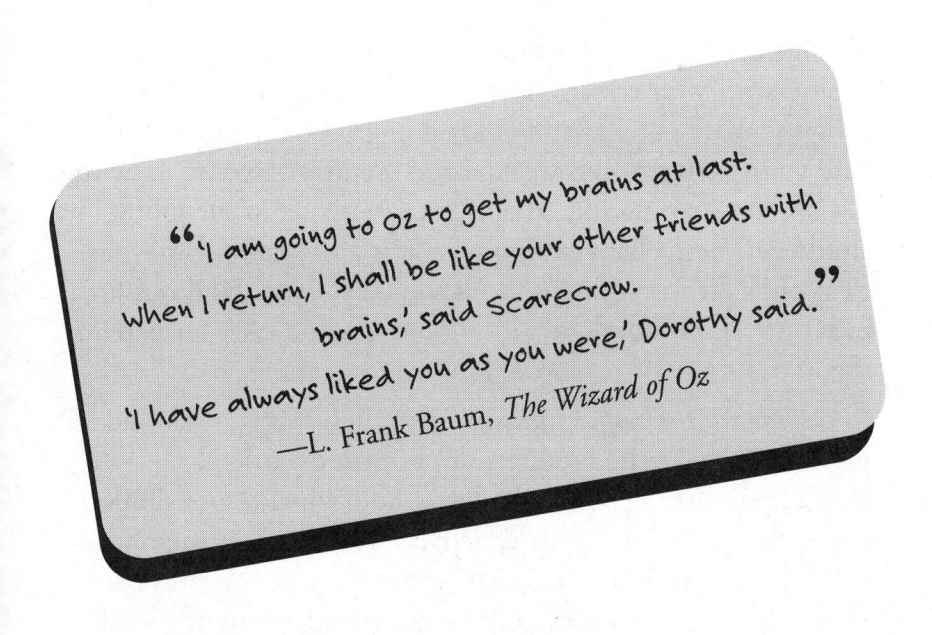

> "'I am going to Oz to get my brains at last. When I return, I shall be like your other friends with brains,' said Scarecrow.
> 'I have always liked you as you were,' Dorothy said."
> —L. Frank Baum, *The Wizard of Oz*

# BUSINESS BUDDIES

*Ideal number of friends: three to five*

If your funds seem to be constantly running on empty, think about teaming up with a few friends and starting a business. Not only can you fatten up your piggy banks, but you're sure to have a blast doing it! The steps below will help you and your friends organize any business ideas you may have. (Some possible businesses are listed on page 56. Pick something that you and your friends all enjoy, or come up with an original, super-creative plan!)

*1. Get permission.* Before you get too excited about making money, check with your parents. Taking on a part-time job is a big responsibility. Be prepared to show your parents how you will budget your time and still accomplish all of your regular chores and school activities.

*2. Plan it.* Once you get the thumbs-up sign, hold a planning session with your friends. Each of you should make a list of the things you are good at and enjoy doing. Use the lists to compare your strengths and weaknesses, then try to come up with a job everyone would like to do. Does everyone in the group love children? Then a baby-sitting service is a natural. Or maybe everyone's favorite thing to do is to make crafts. Find out how to set up a craft booth at a local boutique, or ask your parents if you can go door-to-door selling your creations.

*3. Divide up the responsibilities.* Although everyone should pitch in to make the products or perform a particular service, each of you may need to take on an additional responsibility to get the work done most effectively. On the next page, you will find various job titles, each covering an important task. Depending on the size of your business and group of friends, one person may be able to handle two jobs, or you may need two or three people to handle one job!

**The advertiser** hands out fliers to neighbors and friends and thinks of creative ways to drum up business. This person is also responsible for making the fliers as well as any posters.

**The scheduler** is responsible for setting up a schedule that works for the workers and the clients (those people who pay for your service or product). If one of the workers is ill or unavailable, this person needs to make sure someone can take her place. Otherwise, the scheduler should call the client to reschedule a time.

**The treasurer** is in charge of collecting money from the clients and paying the workers. Some of the earnings should be used to buy any supplies you'll need. If you're decorating T-shirts, you'll have a long supply list, but if you're house-sitting, you may not need to buy any business materials.

**4. *Work out the details.*** At this time, you need to get your friends together and work out any additional details. These will vary depending on your service or product, but here are some basic things to keep in mind:

- How much will you charge for your service or product? (One of the best ways to set prices is to find out how much the competition charges.)
- What days will you work?
- Do you want a business name?
- Do you need to contact your local chamber of commerce for any licenses or permissions?

**5. *Take pride in your work.*** When your first offer rolls in, do the very best job you can. The best kind of advertisement is a job well done. Be proud of what you have accomplished. When the job is finished, you and your friends should celebrate together.

# Brilliant Business Ideas

Below you will find several job ideas for you and your friends to explore, along with helpful tips on each.

## Cleaning

Washing windows, vacuuming, scrubbing bathrooms, making beds, and even washing cars can be profitable. With a friend or two, you'll get a lot more work done in less time.

## Baby-sitting

If there's more than one child in the family, baby-sitting with a buddy can help to even the odds and make the time seem to fly by. (Remember, though, your responsibility is taking care of the kids, not each other!)

## Yard Work

It's probably best to leave heavy mowing to adults with power mowers, but you can still earn money weeding gardens, sweeping driveways, or watering plants.

## Vacation Service

Let your neighbors know they can go away on vacation and not have to worry about feeding the pet, watering the plants, or bringing in the mail. With you and a friend or two pulling the load together, you can either alternate days and duties or do it as a team.

# THE FRIENDSHIP GARDEN

*Ideal number of friends: two*

Growing a small garden is a great way to cultivate a friendship! You and your friend can choose special flowers to symbolize the memorable things you've shared. Your garden will grow and bloom into a living memento of your friendship. (The items you need to provide are in **bold**.)

## The Easiest Flowers to Grow

- sunflowers
- daisies
- cosmos
- marigolds
- zinnias
- larkspur
- California poppies
- sweet alyssum
- geraniums
- black-eyed Susans

## Day 1: Plan and Prep It!

1. With your parents' okay, pick a **small plot of land** in your backyard, about 3' x 4', in a sunny location. (If you live in an apartment, an outdoor planter box will work.) Spend a few hours after school or on a weekend getting your garden ready. Wet the area thoroughly with a **hose** to make it easier to dig. Use a **shovel** to dig up any grass or weeds.

2. Then dig a nice, neat trench, 3" to 4" deep, around the garden area. This will help to keep the weeds and grass from growing back and smothering your flowers.

3. Add some more water to loosen up the soil and let it sit overnight.

## Day 2: Dig and Dig Some More!

4. Use the shovel to turn, or aerate, the soil by digging up clumps of dirt and breaking them up with the tip of the shovel. You need to dig up the entire garden area.

5. Add more water and let it soak in for another night. This will soften the soil and make it easier to work with later.

**6.** Go to a nursery or garden center with your friend to pick up **eight small plants** (two different types of flowers) for your garden. You can always add more flowers later. Make your choices based first on the climate where you live and second on what kind of flowers you like. Planting and watering instructions are available at your garden center.

## Day 3: Plant and Position It!

**7.** You are now ready to plant. With your hands, shape the dirt you've dug up into neat rows. You will place the plants into the mounds of dirt. The lower areas between the rows are for water drainage. Plan on using one or two small plants for every square foot of garden space.

**8.** With the shovel, dig a small hole in a dirt mound you've created, large enough to fit one of your plants. Carefully remove your plant from its container. Try to keep as much dirt around the roots as possible. Keeping the plant in its own dirt will help to prevent it from going into transplant shock. Place the plant into the hole and cover the roots with dirt.

9. Continue until you have planted all the plants. Water lightly with a **watering can**.

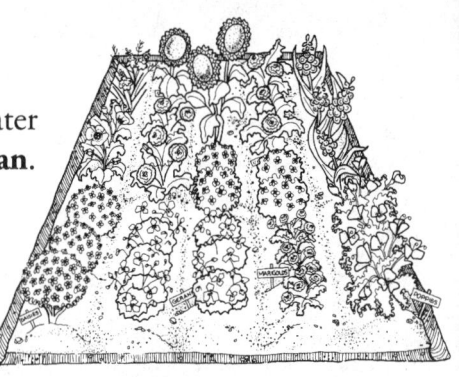

## Day 4: Enjoy It!

10. Now that your garden is planted, you and your best friend can either take turns watering and weeding or do the tasks together. In a few weeks or months, you will be rewarded with big, beautiful flowers to pick, press, and dry for teachers, special friends, or your moms.

### Say It with Flowers!

Whether they're for a gift or a garden, here are some special flowers and what they mean.

Apple blossoms mean I prefer you.
Red chrysanthemums mean I love you.
White chrysanthemums mean truth.
White daisies stand for innocence.
Forget-me-nots mean true love.
Gardenias mean secret love.
Ivy signifies friendship.

White lilies mean sweetness.
Petunias stand for soothing.
Red roses mean love.
Pink roses are for simplicity.
Yellow roses are for friendship.
Blue violets are for faithfulness.
Zinnias represent thoughts of absent friends.
Jasmine stands for joy.

# ACTIVITIES FOR TEN (OR MORE!)

If you have ten or more friends, you've got an instant party. Here are a few ideas to entertain the masses. (The items you need to provide are in **bold**.)

## Pizza Potluck

1. Tell everyone to bring her favorite pizza topping. You supply the **tomato sauce** and **mini-pizza crusts**. Flour tortillas or English muffins work well as pizza crusts, too.

2. With an adult's help, turn on the **oven broiler**. Arrange the toppings on **plates** or in **bowls** on the counter and let each girl build her own pizza.

3. With an adult's help, put the pizzas on a **cookie sheet** and pop it in the broiler until the cheese is melted and bubbly. When they are ready, have an adult remove the hot pizzas.

4. Sit on the floor, break out a **board game** or the latest **video,** and chow down!

## The Bad-Hair-Day Scavenger Hunt

1. Before your guests arrive, prepare a **list of weird and wacky items that relate to hair** for your friends to track down on this scavenger hunt. (See "Scavenger Hunt Hints" on page 62 for ideas.) Make copies of the list.

2. When your friends arrive, divide them up into two teams according to the hair theme. Separate the blondes and brunettes, short-haired and long-haired, whatever!

3. Give each team a copy of the list and set a time limit of one hour. Send everyone off to see how many of the items on the list they can find.

**4.** When both teams return, check the items off the lists. The team that found the most stuff wins. If both teams found the same number of items, the team who made it back first is the winner. The losing team has to give themselves new hair makeovers, using as many of the scavenger items as possible! (**Note:** It's a good idea to wash/clean the items before using them.)

### Scavenger Hunt Hints

Use this list, or add some ideas of your own. Make them as challenging as possible!

- bottle of any temporary hair coloring
- any hair accessory your mother might have worn when she was a girl
- BONUS: 1 point for each doll brought in, each with a different color of hair!
- red curly wig
- frilly pink hair ribbon
- bottle of used-up conditioner
- black comb with teeth missing
- wig with a purple or blue dyed strand (Hint: Girls can "dye" a hair strand themselves with a purple or blue marker.)
- broken curling iron
- three different kinds of hair rollers (pink sponge rollers, steam rollers, spiked rollers)
- pink hairbrush
- rubberband with hair in it
- barrette with ribbons attached
- stretched-out scrunchee (ponytail holder)

> "What I like best in the whole world is Me and Piglet going to see You, and You saying, 'What about a little something?' and me saying, 'Well, I shouldn't mind a little something, should you, Piglet?' and it being a hummy sort of day outside to spend with friends."
>
> —Pooh to Christopher Robin, A. A. Milne,
> *Winnie-the-Pooh, An Enchanted Place*

## Water-athlon

If things are heating up, you and your friends can cool off with this wild water workout.

**1.** Have each girl bring the equipment for one water activity. Here are just a few hot-weather ideas to keep everyone cool:

- Have a **squirt gun** fight.

- Split up into teams and throw **water balloons**.

- Use the **hose** as a jump rope. Each time someone messes up, she gets squirted with the hose.

- Have a Bucket Brigade Relay Race. Divide into teams, then race across the yard holding **cups** of water to see who can be first to fill a **bucket**.

- Play Marco Polo blindfolded, but instead of calling out "Marco Polo," spray the person who is "it" with a squirt gun.

- Have a dance contest in the **sprinklers** (to the hottest music, of course).

- Hold a water-spitting contest to see who can spit the farthest.

2. Put on your **bathing suits,** slap on some **sunscreen,** and go for it!

# Fashion Swap

Everyone has some item of clothing that they're tired of and wouldn't mind trading. (Or, if not, maybe they'd let you borrow it for a while.)

1. Get your mothers to agree that it's okay to swap a piece of clothing with a friend.

2. Everyone selects an item they're willing to part with and brings it to someone's house. Tell your friends also to bring their favorite accessories, such as belts, pins, vests, hats, etc., plus a few basic wardrobe pieces.

3. Each girl picks a number and takes her turn selecting an item of clothing from the "swapping" pile.

4. Once everyone has one new wardrobe item, each girl creates an outfit using her accessories and her fashion savvy.

5. When the creations are complete, each girl can model her new outfit.

Have a **camera** or **video camera** handy to record the results.

# Making a Difference

You and your close friends bring out the best in each other. Together, you can also bring out the best in your community.

1. Choose a project or activity in your neighborhood or community that means a lot to you and your friends. Maybe it's a park that needs cleaning, graffiti that needs painting over, a busy street that needs a crosswalk, or a homeless shelter that is in need of supplies.

2. Write a letter to your city or county officials and tell them about the problem. The names and addresses of local authorities can be found in your city's phone directory. The letter should say exactly how you and your friends feel about the situation. Include your name, address, and phone number.

3. All your friends should sign the letter. If the problem affects a large group of people, you and your friends should ask neighbors, teachers, and store owners to sign the letter as well. (You can attach additional sheets of paper to the letter.)

4. Send the signatures along with your letter to the local officials. You may want to send a copy of it to the editor of your city's newspaper as well. The more people you get to see and understand the problem, the more attention you will get from city and county authorities.

A little bit of work can make a big difference to improve where and how you live!

# BETTER THAN BUDDY BUILDING

If you and your best friends have worked your way completely through this chapter, you have had a lot of fun. You probably know each other better than you ever thought you would. You've been healthy, earned money, planted a garden, showed off your "flair for fashion," and set out to change a part of your world. Most importantly, you've begun forging friendships to last a lifetime.

Don't stop here, though. Come up with your own ideas for things to do, then do them. Don't be afraid to set new trends and get a little crazy. Remember, one of the best things about having good friends is that you can always be yourself around them!

> "We are best friends and soul mates. We're always there for each other, and I know we always will be. She's like a sister to me because she knows me better than anyone else."
>
> —K.M., Tennessee

## CHAPTER 6

# EVERYTHING I EVER WANTED TO KNOW ABOUT MY BEST BUD

*A friend is one who knows all about you and still likes you.*
—Author Unknown

You say you're best friends forever and that nobody knows you like you know each other. But is that true? Do you really know everything about her? Does she know everything about you? Try the following quiz.

## HOW WELL DO YOU KNOW YOUR BEST BUD? QUIZ

Grab two pieces of blank paper and get together with your best friend. On the front of one page, write the numbers 1 through 25, and then answer all the quiz questions about yourself. On the front of the other piece of paper, have your friend write the numbers 1 through 25, and then answer the way she thinks *you* will. Then turn your papers over and switch. Have her answer the questions about herself. Now it's your turn to guess *her* answers. When you're finished, compare what you each wrote to see how well you really do know each other.

**1–4.** Circle four words from the list below that BEST describe you (her):

| | | | |
|---|---|---|---|
| happy | competent | stubborn | loyal |
| funny | messy | open-minded | friendly |
| outgoing | organized | nice | impatient |
| shy | smart | artistic | cool |
| confident | athletic | fair | |

## Likes and Dislikes

**5.** Favorite candy bar:

**6.** Favorite color:

**7.** Worst subject in school:

**8.** Favorite teacher:

**9.** Favorite snack food:

**10.** Favorite movie:

**11.** Favorite game:

**12.** Favorite ice-cream flavor:

**13.** Favorite thing to wear:

**14.** Favorite sport:

**15.** Dream vacation:

**16.** Best feature:

**17.** Worst feature:

**18.** Favorite band:

**19.** Favorite TV show:

**20.** Favorite guy celeb:

**21.** Favorite kind of car:

**22.** I'm (she's) most afraid of:
   Scary rides at amusement parks
   Scary movies
   Any kind of bug or insect

**23.** The thing I (she) hate (hates) to do most is:
   Get up and speak in front of people
   Play team sports
   Clean my (her) room

**24.** My (her) least favorite food to eat on Thanksgiving is:
   Stuffing
   Pumpkin pie
   Sweet potatoes
   Cranberry sauce

**25.** The chore I (she) always put (puts) off is:
        Taking care of the animals
        Putting clothes away
        Cleaning the bathroom
        Doing the dishes

## How to Score:

Give yourself one point for every right answer.

### 18-25
You know her so well, you can practically read her mind. You have a really close friendship and it shows. Keep hanging out together. You'll be surprised how much more you'll learn about each other.

### 12-17
You know a lot about her, but there's still a lot you don't know. Have fun getting to know her better.

### Below 12
Guess your friendship is still growing, and that's okay. You're finding out more about each other all the time.

## SO YOU WANT TO KNOW MORE?

Now, fill out the next few pages with information on your most special friend.

# First Things First

My best friend's full name:

This is how she signs her name (get her signature here):

_____

I call her:

Address:

Phone number:

Birthday:

Birthstone:

Gifts she would flip over:

Gifts I've given her in the past:

This is what she looks like:

(put her picture here)

# Personal Faves

Favorite color:

Types of clothing she loves:

Brand of clothing she likes to wear:

Favorite class:

Favorite teacher:

Who she's got a crush on:

Hobby she most enjoys:

Craft she prefers to do:

Sport she likes to play or watch:

Favorite book:

Favorite movie:

Actor she adores:

Actress she'd most like to be:

Song she loves to sing in the shower:

Favorite tape/CD:

Favorite group:

Perfume she wears all the time:

# Personal Bests

At school, she's tops in:

Her best sport is:

She's so talented when it comes to:

Her greatest achievement is:

# THINK ON IT!

Get together with your best friend and interview each other, using the following questions. You'll laugh, learn, and maybe even shed a few sentimental tears!

1. If you were magically granted three wishes, what would you wish for?

2. Would you rather be an actress, famous singer, renowned athlete, or president of the United States? Why?

3. If you could change one thing about yourself, what would it be?

4. If you were a scientist, what disease would you hope to cure first?

5. What famous woman do you most admire and why?

6. If you could live in another century or decade, what would it be and why?

7. What three places in the world would you visit if you could travel anywhere?

8. If you could adopt one quality from any well-known person, what would it be, and who would it be from?

## INSIDER INFO ABOUT YOU AND YOUR BEST FRIEND

1. What is your most unforgettable memory together?

> "Friendship is the only cement that will ever hold the world together."
> —Author Unknown

2. What is your most embarrassing moment together?

3. What were the circumstances (date, time, place, event) when you two met for the first time?

4. What is the biggest secret you share that no one else knows?

5. What is the one thing you're *sure* you'll do together in the years to come?

# THE BEST FRIENDS COMPATIBILITY QUIZ

Is your friendship a match made in heaven? Take this compatibility quiz alone or with your best friend. Circle the answers that best describe your relationship.

1. Your favorite thing to do together is:

    a) hang out with a big group of people.
    b) go to a movie.
    c) anything! Neither of you cares what you do as long as you're together

2. When it comes to conflicts, you and your best friend:

    a) have never had a misunderstanding; you agree with her on everything because you don't want to upset her.
    b) have your share of fights but manage to patch things up.
    c) have occasional arguments, which usually bring you closer together in the end.

3. When either of you says or does something that makes the other one angry, you both:

    a) ignore it—it's not your place to try and change each other.
    b) ask each other not to do it again.
    c) tell each other how the behavior made you feel and work to resolve the conflict.

4. If you or she were celebrating a birthday, you'd most likely:

    a) do nothing. You both usually have plans with other people.
    b) call each other and offer birthday wishes.
    c) make plans to spend the special day doing something together.

5. **You or your best friend starts hanging out with a new friend, and you now spend less time together. What's your reaction?**
   a) Neither of you cares—you've both got plenty of other friends.
   b) You both have hurt feelings but don't want to intrude on the other friendship.
   c) You tell each other how hurt you are that you are drifting apart, and that you want to do something about it.

6. **Your best friend tells you a secret about her and someone else you know. You:**
   a) tell just one friend—you're sure she won't tell anyone else.
   b) ask your pal if you can repeat the news to someone else.
   c) keep her secret safe—you wouldn't betray her confidence.

7. **You and your best friend have totally different opinions on a particular subject. You:**
   a) try to sway each other's opinion—she thinks she's right, but you know you're right!
   b) disagree with each other but don't make a big deal out of it.
   c) respect each other's opinion even though you don't share it.

8. **When either of you is in a bad mood or has a case of the blues, you:**
   a) sulk, mope, and pout.
   b) still hang out together but try to hide your feelings.
   c) let your emotions out—you both can be totally real around each other.

## How to Score:

Now, give yourself two points for every "c" answer, one point for every "b" answer, and zero points for every "a" answer. Total up the numbers and check out the next page to see how compatible you really are.

## 12-16
FRIENDS 4-EVER! She's an unbeatable buddy! It's you for her and her for you . . . always! You two share common interests and have tons of fun together, and you respect and admire each other. Your friendship's a keeper—hopefully for life.

## 7-11
POTENTIAL PRIMO PALS! She may be a best buddy in the making, but you'll have some things to work on first! Right now you're not as compatible as best friends should be. Maybe trust and respect just haven't been established yet. Keep working on communication and discuss how you can improve your friendship.

## Below 7
OUCH! You two are muddling through whatever you do, and it's not working for either of you. Unless you sit down and talk, this union will be full of ups, downs, and hurt feelings. Try discussing the fundamentals of friendship, like honesty, trust, openness, and acceptance. If you can come together, great! If you can't, there may be another best buddy for you!

> " My best friend is a guy. I can talk to him about anything and he understands. He's the funniest, most understanding guy on earth, and I am so lucky to have him for a friend. "
>
> —M.H., Vermont

# DOES YOUR FRIENDSHIP PASS THE TEST? QUIZ

You've read an entire book on friendship. Hopefully you've learned a lot about what makes a best friend and how you can be a better one. Now check out this quiz to make sure that all your friendships pass the friendship test and that you're being treated the way you should.

1. She never pressures you to do something you don't want to do.

    T    F

2. You know you can tell her anything and no one will ever get her to blab.

    T    F

3. She'd stand up for you if someone was putting you down.

    T    F

4. She helps you out no matter what the problem is.

    T    F

5. She would loan you her new T-shirt to wear to a special party.

    T    F

6. She calls you as much as you call her.

    T    F

7. She apologizes when she's wrong.

    T    F

8. She pays attention to you whether you're alone or in a group.

    T    F

9. She ditches you at lunch.

    T   F

10. She gets mad when you disagree with her.

    T   F

11. She's always competing with you for friends, grades, etc.

    T   F

12. She forgot your birthday.

    T   F

13. You heard she put you down to some of your other friends.

    T   F

14. You've caught her in a couple of lies.

    T   F

15. She borrows things and doesn't return them.

    T   F

16. Your parents don't like her.

    T   F

> "My best friend is always there for me, even when I let her down. She always confides in me, and I know she keeps my secrets safe. She's my support system. Even though we have had our problems, she has never turned her back on me. I know that I am lucky to have her for a best friend."
>
> —J.W., California

# How to Score:

For questions 1–8, give yourself two points for every "T" and one point for every "F." For questions 9–16, give yourself two points for every "F" and one point for every "T."

## 27–32
You have a strong friendship that's likely to last. Your best bud is giving you the respect and support you deserve.

## 20–26
You have a pretty good friend, but she could be a better one. Think about it. Shouldn't a best friend go that extra mile almost all the time? Talk to your friend to see if she's willing to work on your relationship.

## Below 20
Uh, who said this is a best friendship? True friends treat each other better than you're being treated. Speak up. And if you lose this friend, you'll find a more considerate chica.

SHAKY   SO-SO   GOOD   BETTER   GREAT   AWESOME!

> " My best bud makes me smile and laugh all the time. My life would be different (a lot more depressing) without her. "
>
> —E.T., Oregon